CROOKS, COWBOYS, AND CHARACTERS

Sean Price

Chicago, Illinois

Designed by Kimberly R. Miracle and Betsy Wernert
Photo Research by Tracy Cummins
Map on page 4 by Mapping Specialists
Printed and bound in China by Leo Paper Group

12 11 10 09 08
10 9 8 7 6 5 4 3 2 1

Library of Congress Cataloging-in-Publication Data
Price, Sean.
 Crooks, cowboys, and characters : the Wild West / Sean Price.
   p. cm. -- (American history through primary sources)
 Includes bibliographical references and index.
 ISBN 978-1-4109-2695-1 (hardcover) -- ISBN 978-1-4109-2706-4 (pbk.)
 1. West (U.S.)--History--1860-1890--Juvenile literature. 2. West (U.S.)--History--1848-1860--Juvenile literature. 3. Frontier and pioneer life--West (U.S.)--Juvenile literature. 4. West (U.S.)--Biography--Juvenile literature. 5. Outlaws--West (U.S.)--Biography--Juvenile literature. 6. Cowboys--West (U.S.)-Biography--Juvenile literature. 7. Pioneers--West (U.S.)--Biography--Juvenile literature. 8. Peace officers--West (U.S.)--Biography--Juvenile literature. I. Title. II. Title: Wild West.
 F594.P75 2008
 978'.02--dc22
                        2007005964

Acknowledgments
The author and publisher are grateful to the following for permission to reproduce copyright material: Courtesy Colorado Historical Society (CHS.J2239) **p. 5**; Library of Congress Prints and Photographs Division **pp. 6, 12, 16-17, 17, 19, 22, 23, 25, 26, 27, 28**; Bettmann/CORBIS **pp. 7, 8, 11, 21, 29**; MPI/Getty Images **p.9**; Courtesy of the Arizona Historical Society/Tucson **pp. 14 (1134), 14–15** (14835); Alaska State Library **p. 15**; John Loengard/Time Life Pictures/Getty Images **pp. 18–19**; Photo used with permission from Wells Fargo Bank N.A. **p. 20**.

Cover photograph of Annie Oakley reproduced with permission of Library of Congress Prints and Photographs Division.

The publishers would like to thank Nancy Harris for her assistance in the preparation of this book.

Every effort has been made to contact copyright holders of any material reproduced in this book. Any omissions will be rectified in subsequent printings if notice is given to the publishers.

Disclaimer
All the Internet addresses (URLs) given in this book were valid at the time of going to press. However, due to the dynamic nature of the Internet, some addresses may have changed, or sites may have changed or ceased to exist since publication. While the author and publishers regret any inconvenience this may cause readers, no responsibility for any such changes can be accepted by either the author or the publishers.

Contents

Some words are printed in bold, **like this**. You can find out what they mean on page 30. You can also look in the box at the bottom of the page where they first appear.

Opening the West

"Go west, young man."

That was a common saying in the 1800s. A newspaper writer first printed those words in 1851. But many Americans repeated them. Most of the western United States was still not settled. It was a place of wild animals. Dangerous **outlaws** (criminals) lived there. So did Native Americans. People called it the "Wild West."

This map shows the western United States. Little of the West was settled in the 1870s.

outlaw   criminal

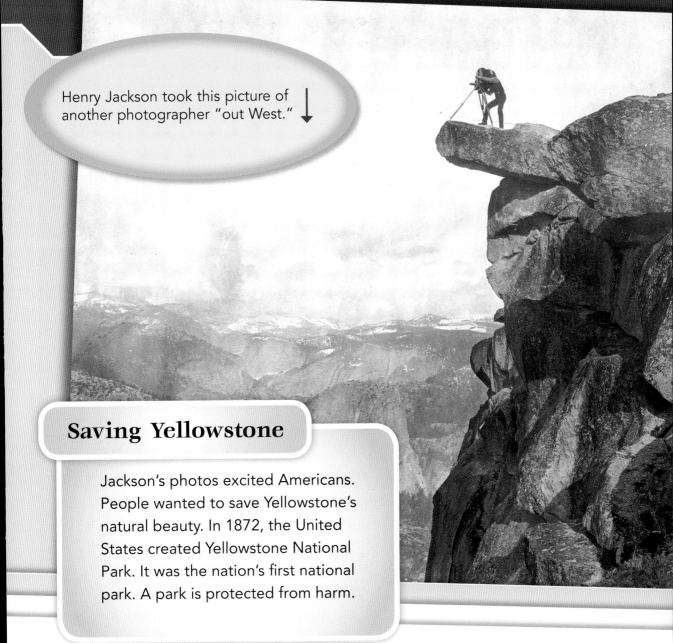

Henry Jackson took this picture of another photographer "out West." ↓

Saving Yellowstone

Jackson's photos excited Americans. People wanted to save Yellowstone's natural beauty. In 1872, the United States created Yellowstone National Park. It was the nation's first national park. A park is protected from harm.

William Henry Jackson headed west. In 1871, the U.S. government asked him to take photos. He was sent to explore the Yellowstone River. Jackson also explored the Rocky Mountains. He snapped the first pictures of these places. Jackson helped shape the Wild West. So did many other people. Some of their exciting stories are in these pages. Read on!

Bad Men and Lawmen

Jesse James was one of the Wild West's biggest **outlaws**. He was a crook. He became an outlaw during the **Civil War**. The Civil War lasted from 1861–1865. It was a war between two sections of the United States. The North fought against the South. James sided with the South. He took part in raids. He attacked towns in Missouri. Many unarmed people were killed.

The South lost the Civil War. But James remained an outlaw. He robbed trains. He robbed banks. He also killed men. Some southerners still liked James. But James was shot in the back by a friend. He died in 1882.

Jesse James led about 25 robberies. He was also very dangerous.

Civil War   war between people from the same country. The U.S. Civil War lasted from 1861–1865.

dime novel   book that cost a dime. It had a made-up story.

"**Dime novels**" told stories about James. These books cost a dime, or ten cents. (But some cost as much as 25 cents). Each was a novel, or made-up story. Yet many people believed the stories were true. Kids loved dime novels. They did not have television back then. Dime novels were fun to read.

↑ Some dime novels told exciting stories about the Wild West.

Billy the Kid was a cattle thief. He was also a killer.

The Lincoln County War

The Lincoln County War was a **feud**. A feud is a long bitter fight. It was fought between cattlemen and businessmen. Both groups wanted to control Lincoln County.

infamous   famous for bad deeds
orphan   child without parents
feud   long, bitter struggle

Billy the Kid

Billy the Kid was **infamous**. He was famous for his bad deeds. His real name was Henry McCarty. But he used the name William Bonney. Billy had a tough childhood. He was left an **orphan** at the age of 14. He had no parents. Billy stole horses and did other crimes.

As an adult, Billy lived in Lincoln County, New Mexico. He became part of the Lincoln County War. Enemies murdered a man whom Billy liked. He killed other people to get even.

Billy the kid escaped from jail more than once. That led him to kill more men. Some said that Billy shot 21 men. He probably killed around nine. A lawman named Pat Garrett finally shot Billy. Billy the Kid died at age 21.

This picture shows Pat Garrett (right) shooting Billy the Kid.

9

Shootout at the OK Corral

As a teenager, Wyatt Earp was an **outlaw**. But Earp later became a lawman in Kansas. Around 1879, Earp moved to Tombstone, Arizona. (See map on page 4.)

Tombstone was a small town. It had many silver mines. People also raised cattle. Earp became a lawman again. He got into a **feud** with some cowboys. It was a long and bitter fight. In 1881, their feud led to the shootout at the OK Corral.

The shootout took less than a minute. Wyatt had help from his two brothers. They were Morgan and Virgil Earp. A friend named Doc Holliday also helped. Earp faced four cowboys. They were Billy Clanton, Ike Clanton, Frank McLaury, and Tom McLaury.

Wyatt Earp was unhurt in the shooting. But the three men helping him were wounded. Ike Clanton was also unhurt. He ran off. But the men helping Clanton died. Shootouts were common in the Wild West. But the shootout at the OK Corral was one of the biggest.

Wyatt Earp was a lawman in Tombstone, Arizona.

COPYRIGHT 1899
RICHARD K. FOX

Annie Oakley was the West's first female superstar. She became famous by shooting a gun. Annie began hunting at age nine. She had to get food for her family. Annie learned how to always hit her target.

As a teenager, she entered a shooting contest in 1875. Frank Butler was a traveling **sharpshooter**. He was a very good shot. He bet that he could outshoot anyone. Annie took up his challenge. She beat him! Annie won the contest. She also won Frank's heart. They later married.

Annie and Frank joined Buffalo Bill's Wild West show (see pg. 26–27). They traveled all over the world. They gave shooting shows. Annie would have someone throw a card in the air. Her shots filled it with holes as it fell to the ground. She once shot a cigarette held by a German prince. Chief Sitting Bull called her "Little Sure Shot."

Annie Oakley was only five feet tall.

Nellie Cashman

Nellie Cashman liked to make money. She lived in Wild West mining towns. People in those towns dug for gold and other metals. But Cashman did not make money digging for gold. Instead, she ran restaurants. She also ran **boarding houses**. People could rent rooms at boarding houses. These businesses made her wealthy.

Nellie Cashman stands in front of a boarding house.

Cashman was unusual for her time. Few women worked outside the home back then. Cashman was special in another way. She always gave away a lot of money. She gave it to those in need. Cashman liked to help people. She once raced to help miners stuck in a snowstorm. She brought them food. She nursed many back to health.

Cashman even spoke up for men **accused** (blamed) of murder. She believed that hanging was cruel. Hanging was a common punishment for **outlaws**. Cashman always lived in tough western towns. Everyone respected her. They admired her good deeds.

accused   blamed
boarding house   place for people to rent rooms to live in

Mining towns like Tombstone, Arizona could be tough places. ↓

Nellie Cashman was known for her good deeds. She helped out a lot of people in the Wild West.

Soldiers and Cowboys

Soldiers were used to keep the peace in the Wild West. They tracked down **outlaws**. They also helped explore the West. Most soldiers were white. However, some were black.

Native Americans called the black soldiers "buffalo soldiers."

Many leaders in the U.S. Army did not like black people. They believed that white people were better than black people. So they separated black and white soldiers. However, many blacks proved to be good soldiers.

Buffalo soldiers had to fight in many battles in the West.

Native Americans called the black soldiers Buffalo Soldiers. This was a sign of respect. The Buffalo Soldiers were led by white men in battle. The Army did not allow black soldiers to have important jobs. But the Buffalo Soldiers fought bravely. They helped show that blacks and whites are equal.

In 1889, some Buffalo Soldiers fought a gang of outlaws. The outlaws wounded many soldiers. The white man who led those Buffalo Soldiers admired them. "[I] have never **witnessed** (seen) better courage," he wrote.

Bill Pickett

Bill Pickett was born in 1871. His family was poor. His father had been a slave. He was one of 13 children. Pickett went to school only until fifth grade. After that, he had to work.

Pickett began working as a cowboy. Pickett invented **bulldogging**. A bulldogger grabbed a **steer** by the horns. A steer is a type of male cattle. Then he wrestled the animal to the ground. Pickett bulldogged in a special way. He bit the steer on the lip! Then he fell backward. That made the animal fall over.

Bill Pickett became a big rodeo star. ↑

steer   type of male cattle
bulldogging   wrestling a steer to the ground

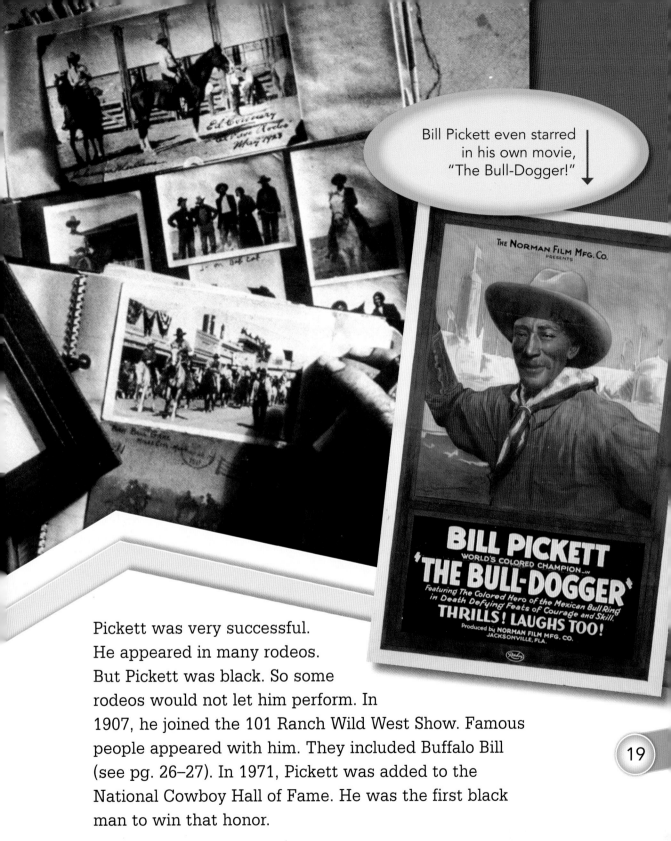

Bill Pickett even starred in his own movie, "The Bull-Dogger!"

THE NORMAN FILM MFG. CO.
PRESENTS

BILL PICKETT
WORLD'S COLORED CHAMPION IN
"THE BULL-DOGGER"
Featuring The Colored Hero of the Mexican Bull Ring
in Death Defying Feats of Courage and Skill.
THRILLS! LAUGHS TOO!
Produced by NORMAN FILM MFG. CO.
JACKSONVILLE, FLA.

Pickett was very successful. He appeared in many rodeos. But Pickett was black. So some rodeos would not let him perform. In 1907, he joined the 101 Ranch Wild West Show. Famous people appeared with him. They included Buffalo Bill (see pg. 26–27). In 1971, Pickett was added to the National Cowboy Hall of Fame. He was the first black man to win that honor.

19

Famous Western Faces

The United States has had only one **emperor** (king). His name was Emperor Norton the First. He wasn't a real leader. His real name was Joshua Norton. But people in San Francisco treated him like a king.

San Francisco, California, was an exciting town in the 1850s. It grew fast. People arrived from all over the world. Norton was a rich man at the time. But he made bad decisions. Norton lost his fortune.

Norton Notes

Norton issued his own money. It was called Norton Notes. People in San Francisco accepted these notes. They treated the notes like real money.

emperor   king or ruler

After that, many believe Norton went crazy. He started telling people that he was emperor. People smiled. They went along with what he said. Newspapers even wrote articles about laws Norton wanted. Theaters gave him free front-row seats. In some ways it was a joke. But people liked Norton.

Joshua Norton named himself "Emperor Norton the First." He wasn't really a king, though.

Eddie Foy

The Wild West did not have movies. Movies had not been invented yet. Instead, people went to live shows, like plays. Most actors traveled from town to town. They put on shows for people.

Eddie Foy became a popular actor in the Wild West. He had acted as a child. Foy made money singing and dancing on street corners. Later, Foy became a comedian. He made people laugh. He dressed up in odd costumes. He sang funny songs. He also starred in funny plays.

Eddie Foy acted in small theaters all over the West. He became famous nationwide.

THE EARL AND THE GIRL
2 YEARS IN LONDON

EDDIE FOY.

Foy dressed in funny costumes to get laughs.

An actor's life was hard. Actors had to travel all the time. Also, Wild West crowds wanted a lot of action. The actors knew they could not be boring. People would yell. They might even shoot guns!

Foy became famous nationwide. He also became a hero. In 1903, a theater in Chicago caught fire during Foy's play. He tried to calm the audience. He wanted to keep people from crowding the exits. His actions may have saved lives.

Quanah Parker

Quanah Parker's name was well known in the Wild West. He was the last of the great **Comanche** chiefs. The Comanches were a group of Native Americans in the West. They were very good warriors. Quanah's father was also a Comanche chief. Quanah was born around 1850. He grew up mostly in Texas and New Mexico. (See the map on page 4.)

In 1867, the U.S. tried to make peace with the Comanches. But Quanah did not trust white men. They had lied many times to Native Americans. The Comanches fought instead. Quanah never lost a battle to the white men. But the fighting wore down Quanah's followers. They finally gave up in 1875.

Quanah agreed to live on a **reservation**. This was land set aside for Native Americans. The reservation was in Oklahoma. Quanah did well. He became rich as a rancher. He also remained a Comanche leader. Most Native Americans remained poor. Quanah used his money to help them.

Comanche   group of Native Americans in the West. They were very strong and brave warriors.

reservation   land set aside for Native Americans

Quanah Parker led the Comanches in war and in peace.

End of the Wild West

In the 1880s, the Wild West was changing. More people headed west. As they did, the west became less wild. **Outlaws** could no longer rob as easily. There were fewer Native Americans. There were more cities and towns.

"Buffalo Bill" got his nickname by hunting buffalo for the U.S. Army.

This ad for Buffalo Bill's show plays off of his nickname.

scout lookout and explorer

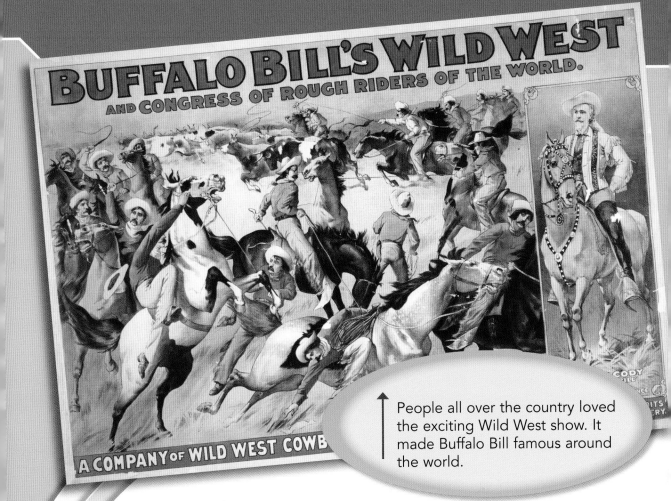

People all over the country loved the exciting Wild West show. It made Buffalo Bill famous around the world.

But people still wanted to see the Wild West. Buffalo Bill helped them. Buffalo Bill had held many jobs. He had been a soldier. He had been a **scout** for the U.S. Army. He was a lookout and explorer for the army. He was also an actor. His real name was William Frederick Cody. Buffalo Bill got his nickname by hunting buffalo.

In 1883, he created Buffalo Bill's Wild West. It was a giant circus. Everything was about the West. Buffalo Bill put on fake battles. They were between cowboys and "Indians." He also had expert shooters like Annie Oakley (see pages 12–13) do tricks. Buffalo Bill became one of the most famous figures of the Wild West.

Tom Mix — Hollywood Cowboy

By 1900, the Wild West was no longer wild. It had been settled. Yet the West was still popular. Movies had just been invented. So movie makers began making "westerns."

Tom Mix became the first top cowboy star. Mix had worked as a real cowboy. He knew how to rope cows. He knew how to shoot a gun. Mix always did his own dangerous **stunts** (tricks). Movie fans loved him.

Tom Mix was Hollywood's first big cowboy star.

stunt	dangerous tricks in a movie
silent movie	early movie with no sound

Early films were **silent movies**. That meant they had no sound. All of Mix's movies were silent. They all followed a similar story. Mix was a good guy. He rescued people. He chased down bad guys and won. Mix made more than 330 movies between 1909 and 1935. Movie fans saw Mix as a true western hero.

Other actors became famous making westerns. They include John Wayne and Clint Eastwood. People still find Wild West stories exciting today.

Clint Eastwood first became famous by starring in "westerns." He has acted in all kinds of movies since then. Today he makes movies himself.

29

Glossary

accused blamed

boarding house place for people to live

bulldogging wrestling a steer to the ground

Civil War war between people from the same country. The U.S. Civil War lasted from 1861–1865.

Comanches Native American group. They lived mostly in Texas, New Mexico, Oklahoma, Kansas, and Colorado.

dime novel book that costs a dime. It had an exciting, made-up story

emperor king or ruler

feud long, bitter dispute

infamous famous for bad deeds

orphan child without parents

outlaw criminal

reservation land set aside for Native Americans

scout lookout and explorer

sharpshooter extremely good shot

silent movie early movie with no sound

steer type of male cattle

stunt dangerous trick in a movie

witnessed seen

Want to Know More?

Books to read

- Isaacs, Sally Senzell. *Sitting Bull: The Story of Our Nation from Coast to Coast, from 1840 to 1890*. Chicago: Heinemann Library, 2000.

- Landau, Elaine. *Annie Oakley: Wild West Sharpshooter*. Berkeley Heights, NJ: Enslow, 2004.

- Zemlicka, Shannon. *Quanah Parker*. Minneapolis, MN: Lerner, 2004.

Websites

- http://www.vlib.us/americanwest/
  Look for links to a wide variety of Wild West websites.

- http://www.pbs.org/weta/thewest/people/
  Find biographies on other great Wild West figures.

Places to visit

- **Amon Carter Museum**
  3501 Camp Bowie Blvd., Fort Worth, TX 76107 (817) 738-1933
  Stroll through the finest collection of Wild West art in the United States.

- **National Museum of the American Indian**
  Fourth Street & Independence Ave, SW, Washington, D.C. 20560
  (202) 633-1000 *These exhibits help explain the Native American experience.*

Read ***Cherokee Rose: The Trail of Tears*** to find out why the Cherokee people were forced off their land.

Read ***Strike It Rich in Cripple Creek: Gold Rush*** to find out why people rushed to the West during the mid-1800s.

Index